Combat Casualty
Caregiver Guide

by Tristan Trubble

Published in USA by:

Tristan Trubble
P.O BOX #9
Boynton Beach
FL 33425

© Copyright 2017

ISBN-13: 978-1546782667
ISBN-10: 1546782664

Table of Contents

Introduction

One of the most troubling aspects of developing a survival strategy is trying to figure out what to do about the medical category. There are quite a few options available to us. Getting a first aid kit should be a top priority. This first aid kit should contain as much medical gear as possible. Stocking up on and storing OTC and prescription drugs and medications would also be a great idea. Researching and developing alternative means for tending to our healthcare should also be part of the process. Essential Oils and herbal remedies are sure to come in handy for long term survival situations and should be something we add to the plan. Most of us already know these things and have made arrangements to obtain these items. Medical guides, such as the one here, are also something we should have available to us, should we ever have to go off grid for any length of time.

This Off Grid Field Medic Guide addresses a number of issues we could all find ourselves facing in a grid down scenario. Most of the material in here deals with injuries and occurrences that are more commonly found on a battlefield. However, as survivalists and preppers, we realize how important it is to include as much relevant information in this category as possible.

One of the things that survivalists and preppers of today are becoming more and more concerned with is the possibility of a war breaking out on the home front. This could be due to civil unrest, in the form of a second Civil War, or it could be the direct result of a foreign invasion. This is a topic most Americans refuse to believe is possible.

They have adopted an 'it can't happen here attitude,' and remain oblivious to the current state of affairs, both nationally and internationally. Historically speaking, America is long overdue for hosting a war within her borders. We have been fortunate to sit atop the throne as a global superpower in the past, but in the present we are seeing several troubling signs that indicate America is no longer receiving the respect she once demanded.

Should America ever find itself in the position of hosting a second Civil War, or the invasion of a foreign force, traditional medical facilities may no longer be functioning. Even if they are operational, it may not be possible to get to them in time to save a life. The techniques and methods we use in the heat of battle, may be the very things that save a life. Additionally, this information may be useful for any number of medical tragedies we come across, under non-combat conditions of the survival nature.

Purpose of this Material:

The information contained here will allow the individual to perform various first aid techniques of the immediate assistive lifesaving nature. This does not mean further medical attention will not be necessary. This information is designed and developed to help the person performing the tasks, stabilize a situation as quickly as possible, preparing the injured for transportation to a better environment for additional medical procedures to be performed. It is a step above conducting first aid by oneself, or in a buddy system, yet lacks in depth surgical procedures commonly performed in trauma/triage centers or conventional hospitals.

This information is something that should be learned, and/or taught, to each member of the family, as well as any and all members of a survival group, or prepper party. The more people in the group who are familiar with these lifesaving techniques, the better prepared the group will be for handling any and all situations of an emergency life threatening nature.

The advantage of having this information and knowing how to use it should be obvious to all. Not all injuries, accidents and events are going to be of the minimal nature, where basic first aid will save the day. The actions we take immediately following such a situation could be the difference between saving a life long enough to get the fallen further medical assistance, and reporting a fatality to the rest of the group. These procedures should only be considered if a more educated medic/doctor is unavailable to attend to the victim immediately, and the injury suffered is of a serious nature, such as stopping massive blood loss, dealing with compound fractures, amputations, partial amputations and chest decompression, just to name a few.

Lifesaver's EDC Gear:

It will be necessary to establish an EDC (Every Day Carry) kit for all those in the survival group who have attained relevant age and understanding. The list of contents for this kit can be found attached at the end of this guide.

As with all other survival related medical gear, it will be necessary to stock up and store enough supplies to replenish those that expire, as well as for those considered a single use item. Whenever an item is used it should either be replaced or sterilized appropriately before being returned to the EDC for future use.

In the direst of situations, such as being caught up in the heat of battle, a gunfight or something of a similar nature, it may be necessary for Off Grid Lifesaver's to replenish their EDC gear in rapid fashion. Under conditions of this type, consider assigning a runner to carry the necessary equipment from the storage area to the area of necessity, all caution and care being given due consideration. In other words don't send a runner to the front line of a battlefield if it is being overrun and a retreat is in progress as this would only increase the potential of reducing numbers by adding to the casualty statistics.

Tactical Off Grid Care:

Tactical Off Grid Care focuses on medical procedures being conducted in a CZ (Combat Zone). Aside from a second Civil War, or a foreign invasion, getting caught in a CZ is still something most survivalists consider a very real possibility. There will be other survivalist groups to contend with, as well as the unprepared zombie squads of average American citizens. Gunfights and battles are a very real possibility!

Historical data from America's previous wars indicates that approximately 90% of deaths occurring on the front lines of the battlefield, do so prior to the casualty being transported to the rear for additional treatment. It also indicates this percentage could be reduced by 15-18% with the usage of proper first aid, buddy aid and the skills covered here. The overall majority of deaths under these circumstances are a direct result of massive hemorrhaging from a limb; an arm of leg.

It is important to note that when under fire, in a CZ, the primary objective is to return fire first and foremost. Attempting to run into an area where bullets, bombs and shrapnel are flying through the air in all directions, a la Hollywood fashion, is not realistic, nor is it logical. Only attended to the wounded when it is safe to do so. If the injured remains capable of mobility, they should be instructed to get to an area of cover and wait for further assistance. Under no circumstances should anyone enter into the arena of battle while gunfire is being exchanged in order to retrieve an injured participant. Survival on the battlefield should remain focused on oneself first, injured and others second. That may sound harsh, but it is a fact. Your survival group will suffer greater loss with each and every downed individual, do not add to the turmoil by becoming an additional combat rescue concern.

Three Phases of Treatment:

Under Fire—the first phase of treatment, occurs on the front line of battle, yet not in the no man's land being fought over. An example would be someone being shot or injured in close proximity to your position; in the same foxhole, or fighting position. Gunfire is still being exchanged in the heat of battle. Medical procedures are limited under these conditions as your focus should be on returning fire. If/when possible, assess the injured and the wound. Primary treatment under these conditions usually amounts to the application of a tourniquet to stop massive hemorrhaging from a limb. Further care should be given once the patient has been moved to a safer location.

In the Field—the second phase of treatment, occurs near the front line of battle, yet not on the front line under direct enemy fire. The area where care is being given could change instantly as the battle lines shift. Medical equipment and procedures under these conditions are also limited and kept to the minimum lifesaving variety.

Evacuation—the third phase of treatment, occurs when necessary. This could be under fire, or after enemy fire has been suppressed. Under these conditions the caretaker may, or may not travel with the patient, depending on the circumstances. If the injury/wound is of a serious and grave nature, and additional medical personnel are unavailable, the caretaker should travel with the patient to the point of getting them to a field surgeon, or other medical personnel, before returning to the CZ. On the other hand, if the injury/wound are stabilized, and/or additional medical personnel of the non-combatant variety are available to assist during the evacuation, then the caregiver should remain on the ground and assist with those still waging the fight.

Chapter 1: Under Fire

Primary Actions:

- ✓ Find cover
- ✓ Return fire
- ✓ Suppress enemy fire (this may be more important to everyone's survival, including those injured)
- ✓ Attempt to prevent injured from receiving additional wounds
- ✓ Determine if the patient is still alive, if possible
- ✓ If still alive and capable, instruct them to remain in the fight
- ✓ If incapable of continuing to fight, instruct them to 'play dead'
- ✓ If the patient is mobile, direct them to cover and have them assess the wound, if possible
- ✓ Relay this information to the others in the group, so all are aware of the current situation

Secondary Actions:

(Note—these actions are to be taken prior to going after the injured patient)

- ✓ Look for signs of danger, the presence of armed enemies or things of that nature
- ✓ Look for and visually assess surrounding structures (a suitable and stable place to possibly use as an area of cover to transport the injured to for medical attention)
- ✓ Plan routes of entry and retreat. Remember to use as much cover and concealment as possible when retrieving the injured, as well as when transporting them to a safer location. Do not plan one route without the other. You may reassess the situation and select a different course once you have made it to the injured, time and conditions permitting, but have one in place in case conditions do not favor establishing a different route
- ✓ If necessary, request and ensure covering fire is provided. Covering fire is that which is intended to keep the enemy from firing back. This will reduce chances of the retrieving party becoming injured themselves
- ✓ Anticipate types and severity of wounds/injuries using best judgment. Were they hit by small arms fire? Were they incapacitated by an explosive device? Were they hit by falling debris, or did they fall from a significant height? Try and determine what type of care will be necessary. Will you be addressing gunshot wounds, broken bones, and/or partial or full amputations? Be ready to apply the proper techniques

✓ Use additional devices for distraction, if possible. In conventional warfare this would consist of hand grenades, machinegun fire, shoulder fired rockets and maybe even mortars. As preppers and survivalists we probably won't have these items, but they may be part of the arsenal of an invading enemy force. Additional equipment for untraditional armament might include Molotov Cocktails, or things of a similar nature. The purpose of this is to provide the retrieving party with a better chance of reaching the injured by keeping the enemy focused on other movements instead of the caregiving process

✓ Assess the situation immediately upon arrival at the injured person's location. Decide what care can be given under current conditions, and what care should be relegated for consideration under safer conditions

✓ In the event there are more than one patient, assessment should be of a prioritizing nature

✓ Determine responsiveness first. Check for signs of life; breathing, pulse and/or movement

✓ Assess severity of wounds/injuries. Will treatment be favorable for saving the life? If so, how much treatment is necessary?

✓ Assign a priority for the patients? Which ones can be saved? Which ones need immediate attention? Which ones can be stabilized immediately and worked on later, as opposed to which ones require emergency attention and treatment within a limited time frame to provide a chance of survival? (Unfortunately it may be necessary to "tag them and bag them," for lack of a better term, especially if there are several injuries/patients, or if they show little to no signs of life)

✓ Treat the injured according to how they have been prioritized. (This will be difficult given the circumstances, especially considering the familiarity we may have with the injured; family members and close friends, but it is something that must be done in order to ensure the survival of as many members as possible)

Checking Responsiveness:

✓ Verbally ask if they are alright. Look for signs of response; audible and visual

✓ Tap and/or shake the subject. Again looking for signs of response

✓ If they are responsive, attempt to ask additional questions focused on the type of injury/wound, and the level of discomfort/pain being felt. This could help determine the appropriate treatment techniques to perform

✓ Ask additional questions of a cognitive nature. This will help determine the level of mental awareness the patient has. Ask for their name, what day of the week it is, where they are geographically, and things of that nature. This will also help determine the accuracy of the information provided by the patient when asked about their injuries and levels of pain. Shock is a very real possibility under these conditions. Patients in shock may be unaware they are even injured. Shock is also a good indicator that the injuries/wounds are more problematic than the patient thinks

- ✓ Use the military AVPU scale to assist you in making determinations regarding levels of responsiveness.
- ✓ A= Alert. The patient gives sound logical replies to all questions being asked
- ✓ V= Verbal. The patient responds to verbal commands, yet does not reply audibly. (Example: They nod their head to respond, or are able to give a hand gesture)
- ✓ P= Pain. The patient is not alert and does not respond to verbal commands, yet when touched near the injury/wound they make sound, or display movement indicating the sensation of feeling pain.
- ✓ U= Unconscious. This does not necessarily mean they are dead, simply unresponsive to all forms of determining consciousness. They may still be alive. Check for other signs of life, pulse and breathing.

Control Bleeding & Stabilize:

- ✓ Check the patient for signs of blood loss. Focus on massive arterial leakage first and foremost.
- ✓ Apply a tourniquet appropriately, over the uniform between the injury and the patient's heart. (More instruction on tourniquet application is provided later)
- ✓ If the patient has a partial or full amputation, apply the tourniquet immediately, even if massive blood loss is not yet apparent. When a body goes into shock from enormous trauma it defends itself naturally, shutting down blood supply temporarily

to the injured area. Massive hemorrhaging will eventually be evident with this type of wound
- ✓ Remember you and the injured are still in an area where gunfire is possible. Do not attempt a variety of methods to stop blood loss under these conditions. Apply the tourniquet immediately. Remove the patient to a safer location before performing pressure dressings to the injury

Evacuation Methods:

(Note: If possible the patient should provide as much mobility as possible for themselves. This will increase the odds of everyone making it to safety and reduce the burden on those responding to retrieve them. That being said it will not always be possible for the patient to assist themselves with mobility)

- ✓ **Dragging**. There are various methods of dragging an injured person to safety. These are a rapid retreat method that are effective for short distances.
- ✓ **One man drag**. This requires a single person of suitable size and strength to retrieve the injured person. Grabbing the garment/uniform, or a strapped on piece of gear, with one hand, the retriever drags to injured to a safer location, keeping their eyes and weapon, which is carried in the other hand, facing the direction of enemy fire. Dragging is the secondary concern when under fire. By using this method the retriever will be walking backwards, capable of identifying enemy positions and fields of fire, dropping the patient if necessary to seek cover and return fire.

✓ **Two man drag**. Similar to the one man drag, using two men grabbing opposite sides of the injured to perform the drag. This is a quicker and easier method of bringing the injured to safety, but it also exposes an additional person to the field of fire, and thus to the possibility of becoming one of the injured

✓ **Cradle dragging**. This is a single man operation. The difference between this and the standard single man drag method is that the retrieving party shoulders their weapon, and grabs the injured in a 'cradling' fashion, beneath the armpits on both sides. This is a little quicker, yet more hazardous method of dragging to safety.

✓ **Carries**. In addition to the dragging methods mentioned above, there are several various ways of carrying an injured person to a safer location. Carrying an injured person means lifting them up off the ground, entirely, or partially. (Partially refers to the injured person's feet being the only thing coming into contact with the ground)

✓ **Hawes**. This is the one all US soldiers are trained in and is the preferred method of moving an injured person from the battlefield using a single retriever. It calls for the injured to be lifted into a vertical, semi-standing position, after which they are draped over the back of the retriever and secured in place by grasping the wrist of the injured in a cross chest fashion. (More information on this later)

✓ **One Man Support**. This is the basic 'shoulder crutch' system we should all be familiar with. You simply throw the arm of the injured over your shoulder and let them use you as a support while making your way to safer ground

- ✓ **Two Man Support**. The same as the One Man Support, only using two retrievers on opposing sides of the injured person being moved
- ✓ **Two Man Gurney**. This method requires the two retrieving personnel to grab the injured by the feet and armpits respectively. This can employ a forward/backward walking configuration, or a horizontal one in which both parties walk facing the same direction.

Chapter 2 - Tactical In the Field Care

This is the treatment given to the injured by the caregiver when both parties are no longer considered to be in the "Under Fire" category, such as in a safer place, yet not in an adequate medical facility. Again, conditions could shift and transition the area into an "Under Fire" category without notice, so medical treatment will be of the immediate lifesaving nature, and not necessarily considered the final solution.

Tourniquet Reassessment:

✓ If you applied a tourniquet while under fire and before evacuation, then reassess the application and results.

✓ **Exposing**. Expose the wound and see if a tourniquet was actually necessary. The injury may not be as bad as originally thought.

✓ **Application**. If the tourniquet was indeed necessary, reapply a second tourniquet. This one should be on the injured person's skin instead of on the outside of the clothing. Placement should be 2-4" above the wound. Once this tourniquet is in place, remove the original one applied over the uniform.

✓ **Tourniquet Removal & Dressings**. If a tourniquet is determined to be unnecessary, use other methods of controlling blood loss, such as pressure dressings, direct pressure, blood clotting agents, and/or elevating the injury above the heart.

Checking for Additional Wounds:

✓ Now that you are in a safer location, conduct a thorough examination of the rest of the injured person's body. Look for additional wounds where blood loss is present and address them appropriately.

Evaluation & Treatment:

✓ In addition to addressing additional blood loss, there are other areas of interest that will require your attention. Continue evaluating the situation and conditions and make proper determinations for treatment.

- ✓ **Airway**. Check and maintain the airway of the injured person.
- ✓ **Chest Wounds**. Look for, identify, assess and address open chest wounds.
- ✓ **Fractures**. Address any fractured bones, splinting them if possible, and securing them in place.
- ✓ **Pain Treatment**. If available provide pain medication, antibiotics, or alternative variants of the same.
- ✓ **Shock**. Identify and treat the patient for shock if necessary and possible.

Relay & Share Information about the Injured:

- ✓ **Communication**. Tell as many others in the party of the ongoing situation. All parties concerned should be kept abreast of the situation, especially in a survival group setting. This information is of vital importance for all involved and could be the deciding factor in whether to keep fighting, or to fall back in retreat and attempt to wait for reinforcements.
- ✓ **Request Additional Assistance**. If there is someone available with better medical knowledge, send a runner if possible and request their presence. This person should be someone not involved in the fighting if possible. If the person is involved in the fighting, then they should be swapped out for the primary caregiver. Use your assets wisely under these circumstances.

Monitoring the Injured:

- ✓ **Recheck Consciousness**. Use the AVPU scale mentioned above to reassess the injured person's level of consciousness. Continue doing this every 15-20 minutes until such a time as they appear to be cognizant and alert
- ✓ **Chest Decompression**. In the event the injured person has an open chest wound, or problems breathing, you may have to open an airway using needle chest techniques. (More information on this is provided in another section)
- ✓ **Documentation of Changes**. Make a note of any changes in patient condition; good or bad. Share and distribute this information among the others of the group. If paper and pen are unavailable, make sure the information is shared accurately with all involved.

Evacuation Preparation:

- ✓ In the event the injured is going to be evacuated to a better, safer environment and further medical treatment and attention is to be given by someone other than the in-field caregiver, then there are a few concerns to be considered.
- ✓ **Records**. Using whatever methods are available, document everything you have identified as an injury/wound, as well any treatments/procedures performed. Make sure this information is attached to the injured so it can serve as a notification to the

individual accepting responsibility for the patient upon their arrival to the safe area.

✓ **Request Evacuation**. If possible and favorable, request evacuation services to be rendered. Depending on the situation this may require the initial caregiver to accompany, or perform evacuation procedures themselves.

✓ **Move & Monitor**. During the evacuation the injured should continue to be monitored, by at least someone with the passing knowledge of battlefield first aid and medical treatment, especially if they are unconscious or incoherent.

Chapter 3 - Examination & Application Techniques

In this section we will cover some of the concepts involved with attending to the injured. These are things you will be performing under extremely stressful situations. These are all areas of interest for the Combat Casualty Caregiver as they apply to actions conducted prior to an injured patient being evacuated to a safer environment, and/or a better medical facility.

Positioning of the Injured:

✓ If/when possible the proper positioning of an injured person under these conditions is the supine position. By placing them on their back you can perform a more thorough examination of the person for wounds and signs of life. Keep in mind that the person may have suffered a spinal, head or neck injury, so caution should be used at all times.

- ✓ **Kneel** down next to the injured on one side of the body, knees touching soil near the shoulders of the individual about to be turned over.
- ✓ **Take** the arm nearest to you and place it out flat above the injured person's head.
- ✓ **Place** the legs of the injured next to each other and lay them flat.
- ✓ **Apply** one hand on the head and neck area of the injured.
- ✓ **Take** your free hand and reach across the body grasping the garments in the armpit area.
- ✓ **Rotate** the injured person towards you keeping the head/neck area in line with the rest of the body. Perform this method as steadily as possible.
- ✓ **Return** the injured person's arms next to the body as they would normally be and lay them flat.

(Note: If the person has suffered a spinal, head or neck injury then this method should minimize chances of creating further injuries to these areas)

Checking Breathing:

- ✓ If the wounded person is alert and breathing on their own, then simply continue monitoring their condition periodically. The purpose of the monitoring is to assure their condition doesn't change for the worse and the breathing doesn't become more difficult.
- ✓ **Head Tilt/Chin Lift**. This is the method of checking for breathing that is commonly used in traditional CPR exercises. This is the first method of checking for breathing that should be applied. If the

airway is blocked by the injured person's tongue, this method should free the airway.

✓ **Look, Listen & Feel**. Once you have performed the Head Tilt/Chin Lift method, kneel down beside the wounded, put your ear next to their oral and nasal passages. **Look** at their chest for signs of breathing; the rise and fall of the chest cavity. **Listen** for breathing sounds; the inhale and exhale of air, and **Feel** for actions of breathing on the side of your face.

✓ **Perform CPR and/or Rescue Breathing.** If the individual is not breathing, then perform CPR techniques, or the rescue breathing portion of them if chest compressions are not possible due to complications with injuries.

✓ **Introduce an NPA (Nasopharyngeal Airway).** There are two situations when a caregiver should insert one of these mechanisms to assist with breathing; if the injured person is breathing on their own, yet remains unconscious, or if the injured person is conscious yet their breathing is troubled, difficult ot sporadic.

✓ **Roll Injured into Recovery Position**. After you have completed inspection of the injured and have determined no further complications or injuries, roll them on their side into the recovery position. This is done by rolling the wounded onto their side. Bend the knee of the upper leg and hook the foot of said leg over the knee of the lower leg. Place the wounded person's lower arm outstretched above the head, bending the lower arm to use as a makeshift pillow, then place the injured person's head on the bent arm, turning their face towards the ground, making sure their airway remains open. The injured side of the patient should be towards the ground or table. *(Note: This position will allow any buildup of excess fluids, such as mucous and/or blood, to continue draining from the oral cavity, keeping the airway as clear as possible).*

Inspect for Fractures:

- ✓ As soon as possible inspect the injured person for fractured bones. A few of the signs to look for are listed below.
- ✓ **Fragmentation**. A portion of the bone can be seen penetrating through the skin.
- ✓ **Swelling & Bruising**. Fractured bones will often cause an area of injury to swell abnormally and bruising should be present. This is usually at the point of fracture.
- ✓ **Deformity**. A fractured limb may also appear to be deformed, yet show no signs of bone penetrating through the skin area.
- ✓ **Immobility**. The injured person may have difficulty, or be completely incapable of moving the fractured limb, or portion of the limb containing the fracture.
- ✓ **Massive Injury Apparent**. If a massive injury exists it may be masking all or part of the signs and indications of a fracture previously mentioned. An example of this might be a shrapnel wound received from explosive ordnance. All evidence may suggest nothing more than a wound, yet a fractured bone could still be present and undetectable until blood

loss has been controlled and further inspection can be performed.

✓ **Reporting of Associated Snapping Sound**. In some cases the injured person may report hearing a snapping sound. If so, assume a fracture exists and proceed accordingly to determine the evidence and make decisions on procedural treatment.

✓ **Splint Application**. If a fracture is discovered, then properly splinting the fractured limb will alleviate pain and stabilize the region until further surgical treatment (setting of the bone) can be completed. To fashion a splint you will need two rigid objects and several strips of cloth.

Leg Splint Application:

✓ **Placement of Securing Straps**. Take the strips of cloth and slide them beneath the flexible bend of the knee. Slide them up or down the leg from this position to intervals appropriate for securing. *(Note: Do not place a securing strap directly over the fractured area as this could increase pain and decrease circulation)*.

✓ **Above & Below**. If/when possible, place two of the securing straps above the site of the fracture, and two below the site of the fracture. Additional straps should be placed above and below any moveable joints, such as the knee or ankle.

✓ **Placement of Poles**. These are the rigid objects used to make the splint. These need to be placed beside the fracture in such a way they immobilize and joints above and below the fracture area. For instance, if the fracture is in the lower leg, the splint poles should be extend above the knee and below the ankle. If the fracture is in the upper leg, then the poles should extend above the hip, (at least on the outer side), and below the knee.

✓ **Padding**. Insert additional padding between the splint poles and all areas of the limb it is being applied to. Additional padding may also be necessary for painful areas, such as joints and knees. Refrain from using too much padding as this could create too much pressure and reduce circulation.

✓ **Wrap the Straps**. Wrap the securing straps around the fractured leg so that the splint immobilizes the area of interest.

✓ **Tie the Tails**. Tie off the ends of the securing straps where they meet. These straps and knots should be tied off against the poles themselves and not come into contact with the fractured limb. Make sure to tie them off on the outer side of the splint poles, this will make accessing and re-securing procedures easier to accommodate.

✓ **Inspect Circulation**. Once the splint is in place inspect the fractured limb for circulation problems. If you notice any signs of poor circulation, such as numbness to the affected area, a noticeable difference in body temperature to the fractured limb, or you cannot detect a pulse in the fractured limb, then loosen the securing straps and retie them. *(Note: The securing straps should be just tight enough to ensure the splint and fractured limb remain immobile, yet loose enough to allow blood to circulate through the region)*

✓ **Evacuation**. The injured person should be evacuated as soon as possible for additional medical treatment and surgical procedures.

Arm Splint Application:

- ✓ **Placement of Poles**. The splint poles should be placed on opposite sides of the fractured arm. If/when possible these poles should extend above and below associated joints. For instance, in a lower arm fracture, the poles should extend above the elbow and below the wrist. For an upper arm fracture, one pole should extend above the shoulder, and both should extend below the elbow.
- ✓ **Padding**. Stuff padding in between the splint poles and the fractured limb. Again, use just enough to stabilize the situation without increasing pain or reducing circulation.
- ✓ **Securing Straps**. The same principle applies here as for leg splints. Two above and below the fracture, as well as above and below the joints to be immobilized.
- ✓ **Inspect Circulation**. This is the same as for leg splints. Loosen and retie securing straps if necessary to accommodate for circulation.
- ✓ **Slings**. If/when possible, apply a sling to the fractured arm and splint. This will help immobilize the arm.
- ✓ **Swathes**. For upper arm fractures apply swathes to help immobilize the fractured area.

Identifying Shock:

- ✓ **Hypovolemic Shock**. This is part of the body's natural defense mechanism. It usually occurs in patients that have undergone serious trauma, such as the wounds being described here. There are several things that can result in hypovolemic shock; massive blood loss, 2nd or 3rd degree burns, and internal bleeding just to name a few. *(Note: Internal bleeding is not something that can be properly addressed or treated under the conditions being described. Do what you can and try to have the individual evacuated as soon as possible)*

✓ **Signs & Symptoms of Shock**. There are several indications that can be recognized and assessed as warning signs that shock is present.

✓ **Sweating**. This will be cold and clammy perspiration.

✓ **Skin Color**. Patients may exhibit a change in the color of skin, becoming paler during the process.

✓ **Blue Hue**. Patients may also exhibit a bluish hue around the mouth area.

✓ **Nausea**. Patients may exhibit episodes of nausea. *(Note: This does not always refer to vomiting, but may include such)*

✓ **Anxiety**. Patients may exhibit episodes of restlessness, nervousness and/or agitation.

✓ **Lack of Cognitive Consciousness**. Patients may pass out, or exhibit a reduction in mental clarity; becomes confused or disoriented easily. The level of consciousness should be checked often, every 15-20 minutes. Patients may seem find during one examination and completely incoherent moments later.

✓ **Rapid Breathing**. Patients may begin to hyperventilate, gasping or gulping for air.

✓ **Dry Mouth**. Patients may exhibit dry mouth conditions, or insist they require more hydration.

Treating Shock Patients:

✓ It is not necessary for the caregiver to witness signs of shock before attempting to treat the individual exhibiting the signs. Shock treatment procedures are also effective means for preventing shock in the first place. One should always assume that shock is present within an injured patient until such a time as evidence to the contrary is determined.

✓ **Shock Patient Positioning**. Place the injured individual in the shock treatment position. The shock treatment position is flat on the back with both feet elevate slightly above the heart. This is intended to improve circulation procedures.

✓ **Ground Protection**. Place a poncho, blanket or other insulating material between the patient and the ground. This will offer some comfort and climate control for the injured person's body.

✓ **Monitor Patient Body Temperature**. Keep a close eye on the injured. Ensure they do not overheat, or become too cold. Make necessary adjustments as warranted.

✓ **Loosen Restrictive Garments**. Loosen but do not remove all tight fitting garments and outwear, boots included. This will help improve circulation.

✓ **Reassurance**. Patients suffering from shock should be given reassurance that you are in control of the situation and doing the best you can to ensure their survival. Refrain from discussing serious injuries or wounds in front of the individual as this could increase anxiety, rather than keep them calm.

✓ **Request Additional Help**. If someone in the survival group has more medical experience, or better medical equipment, send for them. If you must go after help yourself, turn the injured person's head slightly, explain to them to keep that position while you are away, and tell them you will return with help. *(Note: The head should be turned and kept in this configuration in order to prevent suffocation should vomiting occur)*

✓ **Minimal Hydration**. If the individual is conscious allow them to have small sips of water.

✓ **Evacuation**. If/when possible, evacuate the injured to a better and safer medical environment for further treatment.

Avoiding the Shock Treatment Position:

✓ **Unconscious Individuals**. Injured people that remain unconscious should be placed in the recovery position detailed previously. If an unconscious individual vomits, clear the obstructions from the airway using a finger sweep.

✓ **Spinal Fractures**. Individuals suffering from a fracture to the spinal column should be placed on their back. Do not elevate the feet! Stabilize and immobilize as much of the head, neck and spinal column as possible.

✓ **Open Abdominal Wounds**. Individuals suffering from these types of wounds should be placed flat on their backs. Bend and flex the knees, placing the feet on the ground so the knees stay flexed. This will reduce discomfort and pain to the abdominal cavity.

✓ **Open Chest Wound**. Individuals suffering from these types of injuries should be placed in the sitting position against a stationary support; wall, tree, vehicle or whatever is readily available. If a stationary support structure is unavailable, place the injured in the recovery position, injured side towards to the ground. This will allow the uninjured lung to function easier and should reduce pressure to the uninjured area.

✓ **Minor Head Injuries**. Individuals suffering minor head injuries should also be placed in the seated position against a stationary support structure. If such a structure is unavailable, then place them in the recovery position, ensuring the injured side of the head remains up.

Additional Concerns for Shock Treatment:

✓ **Patients with Lower Limb Splints**. If the patient requires a splint to be applied to a lower appendage, then do not elevate the feet until the splint has been properly put in place and secured.

✓ **Temperature Control**. Patients being treated in warm climates should be kept in the shade. If natural shade is unavailable, manufacture it. In cold climates the patient should be kept warm. Use a space blanket or additional methods to ensure they maintain core body temperature.

✓ **Fanning**. Use hand fans to reduce and dry perspiration if necessary.

✓ **Monitor Body Temperature**. Even in extremely warm weather a patient suffering massive blood loss will exhibit abnormally cool body temperatures, be cognizant of this fact and be prepared to respond accordingly.

✓ **Tourniquets**. If the patient has one or more tourniquets do not cover them to the point they will not be easily recognizable upon evacuation to a better medical facility.

✓ **Chemical Containment**. If the injured person is in an area where chemical agents have been used, refrain from loosening any exterior garments as this could result in chemical infections of the wound areas.

Evacuation Procedures:

✓ If/when possible injured persons should be evacuated to a safer location for further medical treatment and care. In a survival situation this may not always be possible. When and where it is possible, there are a few things to keep in mind pertaining to the movement of the injured.

✓ **Preparing a Litter**. This is a two to four man operation and requires a gurney or stretcher to be used. Manufacture one if necessary. Place the injured on the litter in the same position they were placed in while field medical techniques were applied.

✓ **Monitor & Share Information**. If the injured is to be moved and the in-field caregiver is not going to accompany the litter, then make sure all procedures have been documented and passed on with the patient. Assign a caretaker to monitor the injured individual during transport.

✓ **Evacuation of Amputees**. If the injured person has suffered a full amputation, then ensure the amputated appendage is transported with the individual. If possible rinse and remove all debris from the amputated appendage. Wrap the amputated part in gauze. Rewrap in plastic and place in a container to keep cool. **Do Not:**
  o freeze the amputated appendage
  o place it in water
  o place it in direct contact with ice or refrigerated devices
  o place it on dry ice
  o place it where the injured individual can see it

✓ **Caregiver Accompaniment**. If the caregiver is available to assist in the evacuation, they should assume a position on the litter detail at the left shoulder of the patient. This will allow for easier monitoring during transportation.

✓ **Transporting the Litter**. Regardless of whether you are employing a two man, or four man litter detail, the litter should be lifted in unison. Once the litter has been lifted accordingly, the litter detail should walk/march in step to prevent bouncing and jostling of the injured.

Chapter 4 - Controlling Blood Loss

In this section we will be focusing on the proper ways to control blood loss. Massive blood loss on a battlefield, or even just out in the wilderness, where traditional and conventional medical procedures are not available, can and does lead to increased fatalities. Stopping, or controlling blood loss, provides the injured with a better chance of surviving long enough to seek additional medical treatment. If blood loss is not addressed and handled effectively and efficiently, then the patient may not survive long enough for others to assist them.

With a Tourniquet:

✓ The #1 cause of death on the battlefield is massive blood loss. This is also true for anyone stuck in a survival situation suffering from an uncontrolled bleeding injury. Hemorrhaging can often be stopped, or controlled by applying bandages, applying direct pressure, pressure dressings, and elevating the injured limb or appendage above the heart. If these methods fail to achieve the desired effect, then a tourniquet must be applied in order to stop/control the loss of blood.

✓ **Amputations**. In situations where an amputation, partial or full, is present, a tourniquet is required to stop/control the bleeding.

✓ **Under Fire Application**. When the caregiver and injured person are under fire, treatment for stopping blood loss requires a rapidly applied tourniquet. Get in, stop the bleeding and evacuate to a safer location. The RAT (Rapidly Applied Tourniquet) is a simple device. It can be something as simple as a strip of cloth of adequate length positioned above the wound and tied securely in place.

Wound Exposure:

✓ **Under Fire**. When under direct fire, do not expose the wound. Apply a tourniquet over the clothing and in the proper place between wound and heart, then plan for evacuation.

✓ **In the Field, Not Under Fire**. Cut away and remove the clothing in the general area of the wound/injury. Use caution and care, ensure to only cut the clothing, do not accidently increase the severity of the injury by nicking the wound. *(Note: If clothing appears stuck, or burned, onto or around the wound, do not remove this section of clothing, cut or rip around it and leave it attached to the injured area. If chemical agents are* *present or expected, do not remove the clothing, place any and all dressings, bandages and/or tourniquets over the clothing)*

Entry/Exit Wounds:

- ✓ **Checking the Body**. A complete and thorough examination of the injured person's body should be conducted if/when possible. Again, this is not a procedure to be done in a CZ, remove the injured person to safer ground prior to inspecting the body.
- ✓ **Bullet Wounds**. When checking for entry & exit wounds from bullets, it is important to understand and realize that these types of projectiles can enter a body at one point and exit in an entirely different location than one might normally expect. In other words, they do not always travel a straight path. Inspect the entire body, front, back and sides. Identify and dress entry and exit wounds appropriately. *(Note: Depending on the type of projectile, exit wounds may be much larger than entry wounds, they will therefore usually require a heavier dressing/bandage)*
- ✓ **Buried Bullets**. If an entry wound is found and an exit wound is not, then assume the bullet is embedded within the body cavity. Do not attempt to remove the bullet until the injured has been moved to a safer controlled medical environment. Dress the entry wound and evacuate.
- ✓ **Protruding Projectiles**. This area applies to an injury where an instrument/object is still protruding from the body. Do not attempt to remove the object. Apply heavier dressing /bandage around the protruding object and evacuate.

Applying Emergency Bandages:

- ✓ Considering that all members of the survival party should be trained in as much first aid and emergency off grid medical procedures as possible, the combat caregiver should have an EDC kit consisting of a greater quantity of gear; bandages and wound dressings.
- ✓ **Gloves**. The caregiver should, if/when possible, put on sterile medical grade protective gloves to reduce possible contamination from blood borne pathogens.
- ✓ **Apply Dressings**. Apply dressings (gauze pads) directly to the wounded area(s).
- ✓ **Apply Bandages**. Wrap the gauze pad(s) with elastic bandage(s).
- ✓ **Secure in Place**. Once the elastic bandage is fully wrapped, secure it in place. *(Note: If you have an EDC kit with a military grade Emergency Bandage and Pressure Bar, follow the diagram(s) included for proper application)*

Combat Gauze:

- ✓ This is something you should have in your off grid medical gear. It is a roll of gauze consisting of a hemostatic agent. This material promotes coagulation of the blood upon coming into contact with it. Combat gauze applied with direct manual pressure is often used to stop arterial bleeding.

- ✓ **Remove Clothing**. Strip away the clothing around the wound area, remember to leave stuck/burnt clothing in place and apply bandages over it.
- ✓ **Excess Blood**. Remove any and all excess blood from the wound/injury. Leave as much clotting as possible, if any is present.
- ✓ **Identify & Prioritize**. Find and locate the area and source causing the largest amount of blood loss.
- ✓ **Applying Combat Gauze**. Place and pack this material directly onto and into the wound, and onto the source if possible, use pressure. *(Note: The patient may experience pain during this process, it is a necessary procedure, so ensure they are held stable and immobilized to prevent obstruction of the process)*
- ✓ **Additional Gauze**. It may be necessary to use more than one roll of combat gauze, if so then use as much as needed.
- ✓ **Repack & Adjusting**. Combat gauze can be repositioned and packed accordingly to stem the flow of blood.
- ✓ **Manual Pressure**. Applying direct manual pressure for a period of at least three minutes is the preferred method and should produce some level of blood loss control. If it does not completely stem the flow of blood, use more combat gauze and continue applying direct pressure. *(Note: If the individual is conscious and capable they can apply direct manual pressure, if not then the caregiver will have to perform this procedure)*
- ✓ **Pressure Bandage Application**. Once the bleeding has stopped apply a pressure bandage over the combat gauze to hold it firmly in place.

Pressure Dressings:

- ✓ If manual direct pressure does not completely stem the flow of blood from the wound, then apply a pressure dressing. This procedure should only be performed after the patient has been treated for shock and their feet have been elevated.
- ✓ **Padding Placement**. Once the wound has been dressed and bandaged an improvised pressure bandage can be applied to help reduce or control blood loss. Fold up a piece of clean cloth material, (this does not necessarily have to come from the medical first aid kit, it can be a piece of scrap material since it will not be coming in direct contact with the wound itself), and place this over the gauze and bandage, directly over the wound area. Take an additional scarp piece of cloth and secure this in place as tight and firmly as possible. *(Note: Do not use wire or string material as the securing device unless nothing else is readily available as these instruments could cut off circulation and cause additional concerns)*
- ✓ **Check Circulation**. Check the injured person's body temperature in an area directly below the bandage; the area furthest from the heart. If the skin is cool to the touch, loosen the knot and retie the pressure bandage in place. Continue to check circulation periodically and adjust as needed.

Digital Pressure Applications:

- ✓ This is the application of direct pressure using fingers, thumbs, the heel of a hand, or the bend of a knee, to an accessible area of the human body where an artery is known to flow through. This method of applying direct pressure might be of assistance in stopping or reducing the flow of blood so that other procedures can be attempted or applied. The diagram(s) below indicate the major arteries where this type of pressure can be applied.

Tourniquet Applications:

A tourniquet is a constrictive medical device designed for the specific purpose of stopping the arterial blood flow. The tourniquet is a device intended to be used on an extremity, such as a leg or arm. It is not to be used for head/neck injuries or around the torso. Determining whether or not a tourniquet is required is of the utmost importance when assessing an injury.

- ✓ **Extremity Wounds**. If arterial bleeding is present in an extremity, such as the thigh, lower leg, upper arm, or forearm, and you have applied pressure dressings in conjunction with direct manual/digital pressure and the dressings remain soaked in blood, or the blood loss is not reduced to stopped, then apply a tourniquet. *(Note: If a patient is suffering from multiple injuries wherein arterial bleeding is present, the procedures followed may be inefficient for stopping all blood loss. If there are more than one injured person(s) requiring medical attention, prioritize the patients according to severity and address those with a greater chance of surviving their injuries)*
- ✓ **Amputees**. If a patient is suffering from an amputated limb, partial or full, then a tourniquet is required. This applies to all amputees, even if

massive blood loss is not present at the time of assessment and initial treatment. Do not assume that the lack of blood flow from an amputated limb indicates a controlled situation. *(Note: In situations where the patient and caregiver are under fire, or where and when time does not permit additional assessment and medical treatment, a RAT (Rapidly Applied Tourniquet) is the recommended procedure. Additionally, if you are unable to control bleeding by any other means, pressure bandages, direct pressure and dressings, use a tourniquet. It is always better to sacrifice a limb than to sacrifice the life, use the tourniquet!)*

CAT Application:

The CAT (Combat Applied Tourniquet) is a military battlefield medical device. These can, and should be purchased and added to your survival gear, as soon as possible. These units are specifically designed to be applied quickly and effectively under combat conditions.

✓ **Single Hand Application Techniques**. All members should have the knowledge and ability to apply a CAT with a single hand. All members should also, if possible, have their own CAT carried on their person at all times. This will allow an injured, conscious person the possibility of attending to their own wound(s) if a caregiver is not readily available. The single hand application is most often used for an injury to the arm.

  o Remove the CAT from its packaging.
  o Insert the wounded appendage through the loop created by the CAT.

- o Slide the CAT to a position on the appendage that is 2" above the wound site.
- o Tighten the securing strap and attach it back onto itself.
- o Wrap the CAT band around the injured limb. *(Note: Do not wrap this strap over or beyond the re colored locking clip)*
- o Twist the tightening rod of the CAT until such a time as the arterial bleeding ceases. *(Note: Dark red blood may continue to seep or drain from the wounded area for a brief period of time once the CAT is properly in place and tightened).*
- o Insert the twisting rod into the locking clip and secure firmly in place.
- o Check the wounded appendage for signs of continued blood loss or a pulse. If either is present below the CAT, retighten and secure the twisting rod again.
- o Wrap the end of the CAT securing strap around the rod, through the clip and over the entire limb.
- o Make sure the CAT rod securing strap and CAT band are secured in place and continue checking the patient and extremity periodically, making any necessary adjustments required.

✓ **Two Hand Application Techniques**. These procedures are generally used for arterial injuries occurring to a leg. The leg being a larger limb than the arm, more pressure is required to stop the flow of blood. The two handed application technique provides the measures necessary to accomplish the additional pressure required. When using this method, the friction buckle of the CAT is implemented, which is not standard for the single handed application techniques mentioned above.

- o Remove the CAT from its packaging.
- o Place the CAT band 2" above the wound area of the injured limb.
- o Slip the red tip of the CAT band through the inner slot of the friction buckle. Pull tight.
- o Slip the red tip of the CAT band through the outer slot of the friction buckle. Pull tight.
- o Pull the CAT band tight and firm, then secure the CAT band back on itself.
- o Twist the tightening rod with both hands until the arterial bleeding has ceased.
- o Insert the tightening rod into the locking clip and secure in place.
- o Check the injury periodically and frequently for signs of continued blood loss and make any necessary adjustments as required.
  - If arterial bleeding is present, or if such bleeding resumes, then apply a second CAT above the first CAT. Do NOT remove the 1st CAT!
  - Reexamine the injury to ensure the arterial bleeding has stopped.
  - If the application of 2 CAT's does not stop or control the bleeding further medical assistance is required ASAP!

✓ **Improvised Tourniquet Applications**. In the event a CAT is not available for whatever reason, and improvised version of it can be manufactured by gathering a few materials. Improvised tourniquets can be fashioned out of almost any type of pliable cloth material, such as a roll of gauze, muslin bandaging, or even a torn off piece of clothing or uniform. It will also require a makeshift tightening rod, something that can be twisted/turned, and withstand the force applied during such activity.

- o **Gather Materials**. You will need tourniquet banding material. For the purpose of this exercise a 3' X 3' piece of cloth, cut diagonally to form 2 separate and equal triangles. Lay the triangle out, top facing away from you. Grab the top tip and fold down to the bottom edge. Grab the top fold created by the previous action and fold down to the bottom edge. Repeat this step once again for a third fold. You should now have a tourniquet band that is 2" wide and will retain its shape when tightened. *(Note: A belt, the long sleeve of a shirt, or other wide strap, can also be used as the tourniquet band if time does not permit for the rapid fashioning of a cloth tourniquet band)*

- o **Tightening Rod**. Use whatever rigid rod type material you have readily available. This could be a stout and sturdy wooden stick broken off a tree, about the thickness of a broom handle. It should be long enough to extend through the tourniquet bands and be grabbed by both hands on opposite sides of the band itself.

- o **Additional Binding Material**. You will need to cut additional strips of cloth to use as securing straps for the improvised tourniquet.

- ○ **Site Selection**. The improvised tourniquet is applied to the injured limb 2"-4" above the site of the wound/amputation. *(Note: If the first improvised tourniquet does not completely cease the flow of blood, a second improvised tourniquet should be applied 2"-4" above the first improvised tourniquet. Do not remove the first improvised tourniquet)*

- ○ **Improvised Tourniquet Application**.
  - ▪ Wrap the improvised tourniquet band around the selected site.
  - ▪ Secure improvised tourniquet band with a half knot. *(A half knot is created by completing the first half of tying a shoe)*
  - ▪ Set the tightening rod on top of the half knot, vertically and centered.
  - ▪ Secure the tightening rod in place with a square knot. *(A square knot is created by completing (2) half knots)*
  - ▪ Turn the tightening rod (clockwise/counterclockwise). Continue tightening until such a time as the bright red (arterial) bleeding has stopped. *(Note: Dark red blood comes from veins, not arteries, and may continue to flow even if the improvised tourniquet has been applied correctly).*
  - ▪ Check and monitor the injury for signs of pulse below the tourniquet band. If a pulse or bleeding persists, or is present, apply a second

improvised tourniquet as described above.

- Secure the tightening rod in place with at least one additional strip of cloth by wrapping it around the injured limb, then tying off both ends of the strip to one end of the tightening rod. Make sure the tightening rod is secured firmly in place and cannot loosen itself.

- Mark date and time of tourniquet application on the injured person's skin in permanent marker. Tourniquets can be applied effectively and left in place for approximately two hours without creating additional concerns or complications. This information will alert any other attending medical staff of the conditions present upon the wounded person's arrival.

- Apply additional dressings to the wound/amputation. This will help prevent further injury and infection.

- Monitor the injured person and wound site periodically. Under no circumstances should a tourniquet be covered with other dressings. It should remain visible at all times so it can be seen by any other attending medical personnel.

Chapter 5 - Airway Management Methods

Depending on the nature of the injury and additional circumstances an injured person may experience difficulty breathing, or not breathing on their own at all. In these situations it will be necessary to clear the airway and perform certain procedures in an attempt to restore breathing.

- ✓ **Seek Safety First**. Breathing restoration procedures should be done in a safe environment. If the injured is in a CZ they should be moved to safety as quickly as possible before any rescue and restoration techniques are administered.
- ✓ **Use the AVPU Scale**. This was described previously and should be employed to check the patient's level of consciousness/responsiveness and cognitive capabilities.

✓ **Positioning of Patient**. This was also previously described above as the "Recovery Position." Place the patient in this position.

✓ **Open the Airway**. Use the traditional/standard head tilt/chin lift method. Even if they injured person appears conscious and is breathing, this technique can still be employed to assist the person with maintaining air flow.

- o Kneel down next to the injured person's shoulder.
- o Place the palm of the closest hand on the forehead of the patient. Apply firm but gentle pressure in a backwards direction, tilting the head.
- o Using the other hand, place the tips of the fingers below the jawline along the chin and lift the chin in a forward direction.
- o If necessary use the thumb of the chin hand to gently depress the lower lip and keep the mouth open.
- o Inspect the oral cavity for obstructive material; dentures, broken teeth, bile, mucous, blood, bone fragments or vomit. If any type of foreign substance is identified use the finger sweep method to clear the obstruction from the airway.

✓ **Check for Breathing**. This procedure has been previously described. Lower an ear toward victim's oral and nasal passages, while visually inspecting the chest cavity. Look, listen and feel for signs of breathing.

✓ **Procedural Determination**. After checking for signs of breathing the next step is making a determination regarding what actions to take next.

o If the patient is breathing on their own, is conscious and responsive, then monitor respiratory rate for a period of at least 15 seconds. If the patient exhibits less than two full respirations within the 15 second time frame, then insert an NPA (Nasopharyngeal Airway) if available. *(Note: This is an item that may need to be purchased separately if current First Aid and medical gear do not contain them)* then set the patient in the Recovery Position.

o For patients who are breathing on their own, are conscious and responsive, yet have a guttural/snoring noise associated with their breathing, insert the NPA and set patient in Recovery Position.

o For unconscious/unresponsive patients, insert NPA and use the Recovery Position.

o For patients that are not breathing on their own, and who do not have an open chest wound, check for a pulse along the carotid artery. If a pulse is identified begin performing CPR/rescue breathing techniques. If no pulse is identified, discontinue rescue efforts.

o For patients who are not breathing, or attempting to breathe on their own, and who have an open chest wound present, treatment is unlikely to produce favorable results. If there are more than one wounded, treat others with clear vital signs first.

✓ **Rescue Breathing Techniques**. These should only be attempted if there are no other injured people, or if those injured people are being properly attended to by someone with sufficient medical knowledge and equipment. With rescue breathing, the caregiver blows air through the injured person's mouth and into the lungs. The caregiver then allows the air to be expelled. This replicates the human body's natural breathing exercise.

- o Kneel down next to the injured person near the shoulder area.
- o With the injured person in the head tilt/chin lift position, pinch the nasal passages closed.
- o Open your mouth and inhale deeply.
- o Keeping your mouth open wide, place yours over theirs, ensure a good seal is created and blow forcefully.
- o Attempt to visually inspect the injured person's chest cavity during the process. If air is making its way into the injured person's lungs the chest should rise.
- o Release your pinch on the nasal passages and allow air to expel. Visually inspect the chest area here as well, it should fall.
- o Evaluate the effects of the rescue breathing attempt. If the patient's chest rose and fell as expected, then continue the rescue breathing efforts, one breath for every 5 seconds. If the patient's chest did not rise and fall as expected, make sure the head tilt/chin lift position has not been compromised. Reexamine the airway for obstructive material and remove. Repeat initial rescue breathing attempt and reevaluate effects. If the chest rises and falls continue rescue breathing efforts, one breath every 5 seconds. If chest fails to rise and fall,

discontinue efforts and attend to other injured individuals first.

o Check the patient's carotid pulse every 60 seconds. Examine and inspect the injured person while performing this procedure to see if they have begun, or are continuing to breathe on their own.

✓ **Checking the Carotid Artery for Pulse**.

o Place the palm of your hand on the forehead of the patient to maintain a clear airway.

o Locate one of the carotid arteries. This can be done on either side of the patient's neck, use the side closest to your location. Feel for one on either side of the windpipe, where the groove is located.

o Using your first and second fingers of the hand that is free, find the artery and check for a pulse. Continue checking for 5-10 seconds.

o Evaluate and determine appropriate actions as needed.

  ▪ If a pulse is present, yet the patient is not breathing on their own, then continue rescue breathing efforts, checking the carotid artery every 60 seconds.

  ▪ If no pulse is present and the patient is not breathing on their own, CPR procedures can be implemented so long as all other concerns have been met, and all other patients have been attended to, otherwise rescue efforts should be ceased to maximize medical attention where it may be more effective at saving a life.

- If there is a pulse and the patient is capable of breathing on their own, evaluate and determine if an NPA insertion is required, or would be assistive for helping the patient breathe.
- Continue rescue breathing and CPR efforts as necessary, or until such a time as a determination they are ineffective has been made.

✓ **Inserting an NPA**. An NPA is a specially designed medical device. It may need to be purchased separately if not part of your First Aid Kit contents. This device is intended to be inserted through one of the patient's nasal passages to maintain an open airway while preventing the patient's tongue from falling/folding back on itself and blocking the throat. (*Note: An NPA should not be inserted if the patient has had head trauma, has head trauma currently, the roof of the oral cavity is broken, or if there is brain matter visible from the patient's own head. An NPA should also not be used if there is the presence of clear fluid seeping from the ears or nasal passages of the patient as this could indicate a skull fracture*)

- o Place the patient on their back, face up.
- o Lubricate the tubular end of the NPA with medical grade lubricant or water if nothing else is readily available.
- o Using a thumb and forefinger grasp the tip of the patient's nose and tilt it up/back, exposing the nasal passage.

- o Insert the tip of the NPA tube into the nasal passage.
- o Rotate the NPA tube if necessary to align the pointed end with the inside dividing wall of the nose.
- o Continue sliding/inserting the NPA until the flange of the device is resting against the nostril.
- o Secure the NPA in place with a piece of tape, and instruct the patient to leave it alone, restrain their arms and hands if necessary. Otherwise place them in the Recovery Position.

    (Note: Do not force the NPA insertion procedure. If the NPA insertion is met with resistance or encounters an obstruction remove it from the current nasal passage and attempt the procedure in the patient's other nasal passage. If both are obstructed discontinue attempting to insert an NPA)

✓ **Recovery Position**. The proper positioning for a patient being situated in the Recovery Position is depicted below.

Chapter 6 - Penetrating Chest Trauma Treatment

The human body has two lungs, each contained in its own airtight environment within the chest cavity. These airtight environments are under constant and consistent negative pressure when the body is operating/functioning normally. If the wall of the chest cavity is punctured, outside air could be allowed to enter the area. If the puncture is deep enough to penetrate/puncture one of these previously airtight environments, the lung within it will begin to collapse. It is possible for one or both airtight environments to be compromised from a single penetration/puncture wound. However, any compromise of either airtight environment will introduce interference with the patient being able to breathe. It will also reduce the quantity of oxygen available for the patient's body to use. In most cases the lung(s) will not collapse immediately, although it may seem as they have given the patient's response to the situation. They will however continue to collapse as more outside air is introduced to the previous airtight environment. This creates a positive pressure condition and restricts, reduces or prohibits the lung(s) from expanding as they would normally.

✓ **Signs, Symptoms and Signals of an Open Chest Wound**. There are a number of things that could cause a penetration of the chest cavity wall and airtight environment around the lungs, especially if the injured person was directly involved in a CZ and received injuries due to fighting. Bullets, shrapnel, a knife blade, bayonet, makeshift spear or other device could be the introducing instrument of the penetration/puncture wound. *(Note: When unsure if a chest wound has penetrated the airtight environment around the lungs, treat the wound as if it has)*

  o Sucking/hissing sounds when the patient attempts to breathe are a good indication the airtight environment(s) has/have been penetrated.

  o A patient that coughs up blood also exhibits signs of an open chest wound.

  o A bubbly/frothy blood/air mixture is present in, or around the chest wound.

  o Difficulty or distress while trying to breathe, rapid inhalations, gasping for air.

  o Chest does not rise and fall normally.

  o Increased sensation of pain in the chest or shoulder areas when the patient attempts to inhale.

  o A bluish hue present in the oral area, including lips, tongue and inner cheek linings, and/or in the fingertips, or the fingernail beds.

- o Signs indicating shock such as a rapid or faint heartbeat.
- ✓ **Checking for Chest Wounds**. Inspect the patient thoroughly, identifying all entry/exit wounds. If more than one penetrating/puncturing chest wound is present, attend to the first one you come across, unless the severity of another calls for immediate attention. Do not attempt to wash/rinse away blood, use your hands and fingers to search for and find wounds.
- ✓ **Exposing the Wound Area**. This area was covered previously but warrants repetition in this category. Cut, rip or tear clothing away from the wound site, leaving any burnt or otherwise stuck fabric in place. If objects are still present, or protruding from the wound, do not attempt to remove them, apply dressings and bandages around and over the wound leaving the protrusion to be removed at a later time.
- ✓ **Sealing the Chest Wound**. In order to properly and effectively seal an open chest wound the use of nonporous material must be used; plastic, Saran wrap, cellophane or something of a similar nature should be used. Gauze, bandages and cloth fabric are breathable and will not suffice for sealing off an open chest wound. This nonporous material will stabilize the airtight environment until further surgery can be completed.
    - o Put on protective neoprene gloves if available, and time and conditions permit. This will reduce the chance of contamination from blood borne pathogens.
    - o Prepare the nonporous plastic patches. Each entry/exit wound will need its own plastic patch. These should be cut and fabricated to

extend 2" on all sides of the wound hole. These patches must also be able to lie flat against the skin of the patient, so make sure flexibility is a characteristic of the material being used.

o   Instruct the patient to exhale as much air as possible out of their chest cavity and to hold their breath as long as possible. The more air that can be expelled from the area, the better the patient should be able to breathe once the entry/exit wounds are properly sealed. *(Note: Conscious patients may resume normal breathing upon completion of the wound seal. If a patient is unconscious/unresponsive, wait for the chest area to deflate and time sealing the wound during this event, before the patient inhales again).*

o   Apply the plastic sealing patch directly over the wound. Inspect the positioning of the plastic patches ensuring a 2" minimum clearance is achieved from the all edges of the wound, reposition if necessary by sliding. Do not remove and reapply unless the original patch is insufficient in size and shape. Make sure none of the edges have been sucked inside the wound.

o   Secure the plastic in place over the wound, use medical grade tape, or wrap a roll of gauze or bandage around the entire torso and tie in place directly over the plastic seal patch.

o   Once the airtight patch has been secured in place, set the patient in the Recovery Position. If the patient is conscious and is able to breathe easier by sitting up, then allow them to do so, using a stationary back support to lean against.

Chapter 7 - Tension Pneumothorax Treatment

This condition happens when too much air is allowed to enter the airtight environment around one or both lungs. This area is known medically as the plural space. As mentioned early it is normally a negative pressure environment, however when an open chest wound introduces air from outside the body to this space, the negative pressure converts to a positive pressure field. The buildup of air in this area will cause the affected lung to continue collapsing. If left untreated it can eventually begin to cause problems with the other lung and its plural space, as well as restrict blood vessels and create a compression of the uninjured lung itself.

✓ **Signs & Symptoms of Pneumothorax.** Some of the warning signs and recognizable symptoms that a patient is suffering from pneumothorax conditions are as follows:

- o **Anxiety**
- o **Apprehension**
- o **Agitated**
- o **Distressed/Shorter Breathing Sounds**
- o **Bluish Hue at lips, mouth, fingertips and/or base of fingernails**
- o **Rapid Short Breathing**
- o **Engorged Veins in Neck Area**
- o **Low Blood Pressure/Loss of Radial Pulse**
- o **Cold & Clammy Skin**
- o **Decreased level of consciousness/responsiveness or cognitive capabilities**
- o **Physical Deterioration of a visible nature**
- o **The patient suddenly loses consciousness or passes out**
- o **Windpipe is shifted to the left/right abnormally**

✓ **Needle Chest Decompression Technique**. This is the recommended treatment for relieving Tension Pneumothorax and is performed when the patient has increased difficulty breathing in conjunction with serious upper torso trauma.

✓ **Materials Required**.
   - o 14 gauge large bore needle/catheter 3-1/4" in length. *(Note: If your First Aid kit or medical gear does not come stocked with this item you may need to purchase separately)*
   - o Alcohol Pad
   - o Tape

✓ **Insertion Site Identification**. The location for inserting the needle chest decompression catheter can be found on either side of the human body. When performing this procedure it should be conducted on the same side of the body as the injury. The medical technical language for locating this position can be confusing for those not familiar with the terms. In basic laymen's terms the insertion site is located between the 2nd and 3rd ribs counting from the top down below the clavicle and along an imaginary line that runs vertically in line with the patient's nipple. *(Note: The easiest way to find the proper spot is by putting the first and second fingers of a hand together. Place these two finger beneath the patient's clavicle. The tip of the needle/catheter goes below these two fingers along the imaginary nipple line)*

✓ **Sterilize the Site**. Once you have located the site properly, use the alcohol pad (Isopropyl) and sterilize the area by cleaning it thoroughly.

✓ **Insertion**. Take the needle/catheter and insert it firmly into the proper location at a 90^0 angle. Make sure to insert just above the 3rd rib rather than directly underneath the 2nd rib. This will help protect the blood vessels present there and prevent further complication. Always ensure the needle/catheter are not aimed towards the heart. Continue pushing the needle/catheter until the hub is reached. If performed correctly an audible popping noise should be heard, as well as the hissing sound of air escaping through the needle/catheter.

✓ **Withdrawal**. Remove the needle portion while maintaining the catheter in place.

✓ **Secure Catheter**. Use medical tape to secure the catheter in place. Make sure not to cover the opening of the catheter in the process.

✓ **Monitoring**. Once performed the patient should be monitored frequently. If the needle chest decompression catheter was inserted properly and is performing as intended the patient should realize almost immediate relief and less difficulty breathing. Continue to monitor the patient until further medical treatment can be given, or until the can be evacuated. If shock is present, or appears, treat accordingly.

✓ **Transporting the Patient**. In the event a patient treated for Tension Pneumothorax with a needle chest decompression kit needs to be moved, they should be transported with their injured side down. If the patient is alert and prefers a sitting position for comfort, then ensure they are supported.

Chapter 8 - Documentation

Documenting the injuries and procedures taken is of vital importance and for many reasons. Considering that this material is intended to be used as initial trauma care for a patient suffering an injury of the battlefield nature, and in conjunction with a survival atmosphere of the unconventional kind, documentation of events may have to be modified. A medical log of some sort should always be kept for the patient. This information should include, but is not limited to;

- ✓ Name of Patient
- ✓ Age (if known)
- ✓ Date
- ✓ Time
- ✓ Type of Injury
- ✓ Extent of Injury (Level of severity as determined by the onsite caregiver)

- ✓ Treatment Procedures (detailed)
- ✓ Vital Signs (Heart Rate/Pulse; Blood Pressure; etc., if taken and if possible)
- ✓ Name of Caregiver

This information should be kept with the patient at all times and if the patient is to be transported the information documents should travel with the patient. Clear, concise and legible writing should be applied to prevent confusion and complications with understanding and determining further action. If communications are available, include contact information for the caregiver so that future medical personnel may get ahold of them if necessary. This more than likely will not be possible, but if it is, make sure to include it. Use permanent marker when possible to prevent deterioration of the information contained in the document.

Conclusion

The material provided in this guide reflect emergency procedures to be performed by an individual with limited medical knowledge, education and equipment. These are life saving techniques that have been designed and developed to utilize minimal procedures and equipment. In almost all cases the patient is going to need further medical attention and possibly even surgical procedures. Do not assume that these procedures are the final solution. The environment in which these medical procedures are performed is extremely stressful and time is of the essence.

These medical procedures should be practiced using a variety of simulated scenarios without actually performing them unnecessarily. In other words, do not actually perform a chest needle compression techniques on an *acting* patient, as this would obviously result in complications requiring a visit to the nearest hospital. Practicing these techniques will get you familiar with the generalized principles and procedures. However, classroom environments are seldom capable of replicating what a caregiver might come across in a real world setting.

The majority of the equipment mentioned in this guide is standard in military medical gear kits. These can be purchased online as well as from a number of survival stores and outlets. These kits are commonly referred to as Combat Lifesaver Medical Equipment Sets. The equipment, instructions and procedures listed here are also standard military battlefield applications. As such the primary focus of this material is intended to guide the caregiver through the proper steps and procedures of attending to various injuries, stabilizing them and preparing the patient to be evacuated for further treatment.

Considering that the majority of survival situations will involve very limited resources in the form of medical procedures, equipment and personnel, additional treatment and care may not be readily available. The techniques described in this guide may help save a person's life initially, however if further treatment is not obtainable, the life being saved could be of the temporary nature. It is highly recommended that as many people as possible, within your survival group, be trained in a wide variety of off grid medical procedures. Surgical solutions should only be performed by those with proper training. All members of the survival group, of relative age, should be properly trained in the various steps and procedures outline in this guide.

Improvised litters can be fashioned out of a wide variety of unconventional equipment and should be used whenever possible for transporting an injured person. Litters distribute the weight of the injured patient better and allow for easier transportation techniques to be applied. Litters and stretchers can purchased and included in the survival gear, or they can be made from something as simple as two poles and a blanket, or two poles and a couple of jackets. Whenever possible do not move an injured person unnecessarily. Patient's suffering injuries should be immobilized as much as possible until such a time as they can be properly stabilized, treated and deemed fit for movement. Evacuation will almost always be necessary and should be done in the safest manner possible.

DISCLAIMER AND/OR LEGAL NOTICES: Every effort has been made to accurately represent this book and it's potential. Results vary with every individual, and your results may or may not be different from those depicted. No promises, guarantees or warranties, whether stated or implied, have been made that you will produce any specific result from this book. Your efforts are individual and unique, and may vary from those shown. Your success depends on your efforts, background and motivation.

The material in this publication is provided for educational and informational purposes only and is not intended as medical advice. The information contained in this book should not be used to diagnose or treat any illness, metabolic disorder, disease or health problem. Always consult your physician or health care provider before beginning any nutrition or exercise program. Use of the programs, advice, and information contained in this book is at the sole choice and risk of the reader.